Rhymes
of the
Raven Lady

In our legends
there is Raven
in times of trouble he was
the hero
in times of smiles he was
the Trickster
in ancient times and even
now
when there is darkness
Raven is the Bringer of
Light

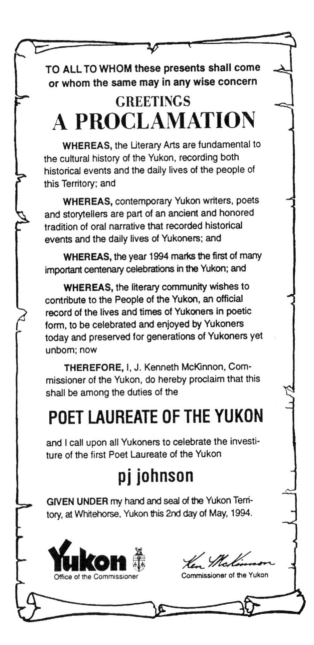

**TO ALL TO WHOM these presents shall come
or whom the same may in any wise concern**

GREETINGS

A PROCLAMATION

WHEREAS, the Literary Arts are fundamental to
the cultural history of the Yukon, recording both
historical events and the daily lives of the people of
this Territory; and

WHEREAS, contemporary Yukon writers, poets
and storytellers are part of an ancient and honored
tradition of oral narrative that recorded historical
events and the daily lives of Yukoners; and

WHEREAS, the year 1994 marks the first of many
important centenary celebrations in the Yukon; and

WHEREAS, the literary community wishes to
contribute to the People of the Yukon, an official
record of the lives and times of Yukoners in poetic
form, to be celebrated and enjoyed by Yukoners
today and preserved for generations of Yukoners yet
unborn; now

THEREFORE, I, J. Kenneth McKinnon, Com-
missioner of the Yukon, do hereby proclaim that this
shall be among the duties of the

POET LAUREATE OF THE YUKON

and I call upon all Yukoners to celebrate the investi-
ture of the first Poet Laureate of the Yukon

pj johnson

GIVEN UNDER my hand and seal of the Yukon Terri-
tory, at Whitehorse, Yukon this 2nd day of May, 1994.

Yukon
Office of the Commissioner

Commissioner of the Yukon

*"Special thanks to the Canada Council & Yukon Lotteries; to
Audrey McGloughlin, Jane Urquart, and Nino Ricci for their
support and encouragement, and to Roch Carrier who said, "Just
be yourself."*

Rhymes
of the
Raven Lady

pj johnson
Yukon Poet Laureate

Illustrations
Wm. C. Sinclair

hancock

house

ISBN 0-88839-366-0
Copyright © 1995 pj johnson

Cataloging in Publication Data
Johnson, P.J., 1950-
    Rhymes of the raven lady

    ISBN 0-88839-366-0

    I. Title
PS8569.O5R59 1995   C811'.54   C95-910170-5
PR9199.3.J63R59 1995

Production: Tom Pardy and Myron Shutty
Cover painting: Wm. C. Sinclair

Published simultaneously in Canada and the United States by

HANCOCK HOUSE PUBLISHERS LTD.
19313 Zero Avenue, Surrey, B.C. V4P 1M7
(604) 538-1114   Fax (604) 538-2262

HANCOCK HOUSE PUBLISHERS
1431 Harrison Avenue, Blaine, WA 98230-5005
(604) 538-1114   Fax (604) 538-2262

Contents

Never in My Wildest Dreams....

In the early 1980's I once had a job working as a janitor at the Robert Service School in Dawson City. Back in those days I was a busy single parent raising four children, struggling desperately to keep the wolf away from our door. Looking back I sometimes wonder how we all survived.

The town of Dawson, located 330 miles north of Whitehorse at the confluence of the Klondike and Yukon rivers, once boasted a population of 30,000 at the height of her fame during the Klondike Gold Rush. Today a ghost town of about 900, the entire city has been designated as a national historic site.

Something I found enchanting about Dawson City is the fact that the town has also served as home to several world-famous authors. Directly across the street from the house we lived in was an old miner's cabin that once belonged to Jack London (and which my children often used as a playhouse), from my bedroom window I could see Robert Service's tiny tree-framed cabin a few yards down the street, and as I walked to work each day I often passed by the stately old Berton Home where Canadian author Pierre Berton spent his childhood.

My job at the school involved a lot of back-breaking labor and often seemed a rather thankless task but I was fascinated by the world of education. Perhaps this was partly due to the fact that my own personal journey into that hallowed system had scarcely taken me as far as junior high.

One of my favorite places in the school was the library where I often took a break from my never-ending vacuming to thumb through the odd book. I remember spending the better part of an hour one afternoon—with one eye on the door in case the boss was hovering, totally engrossed in a book about Bibles—absolutely amazed that somebody would sit down and write an entire book about them. Apparently there are over 200 different kinds, including something called a Tree Bible.

Although my job was menial it was not entirely without perks. With the focus on physical labor, my mind was free to wander and I often took little mind trips to help pass the time and break the monotony.

Occasionally as I mopped the floor of the school gymnasium I would glance over at the stage and picture myself there— dressed in an elaborate costume as I played the lead role in a smash-hit Shakespeare production. Other times I might be an exotic chanteuse, softly crooning ballads before a rapt audience, bowing most graciously at the conclusion of yet another flawless performance as the sound of thunderous applause shook the building.

But perhaps my favorite daydream was inspired by the fact that I was more than a little intrigued by the name of the school itself. Robert Service, world-famous bard of the North... and sometimes as I scrubbed and scoured toilets in the building named in his honor, I imagined him looking down, smiling and nodding his approval.

But though I often entertained myself with some truly incredible flights of fantasy over the course of my career as a school janitor, never in my wildest dreams, as I scraped gum and spitballs from the walls of Robert Service School, did I imagine that I was destined to one day become the first Poet Laureate of the Yukon.

The Story of the Yukon Raven Lady

by Ken Spotswood

Mention the word 'controversy' in the Yukon and what comes to mind? The storm that erupted in 1985 over the campaign to make the northern raven the Yukon's official territorial bird.

At the eye of this storm was Yukon poet pj johnson. These days she's popularly known throughout the Yukon territory as the Raven Lady, the woman who single-handedly took on the government—and won.

So why all the fuss over a bird? For starters, the raven isn't any ordinary bird. How many creatures do you know that can walk around in bare feet when it's minus fifty outside, and still get their kicks from dive-bombing the neighbor's Husky?

How many birds have the cunning to tip off predators to game, just so they can feed on the leftovers?

The raven can mimic human speech as well as the jake brake of a semi truck. They can unfasten the safety pin that locks a construction worker's lunch box, and their sharp beaks make short work of things like $500 tents.

The raven was immortalized in the Bible by being the first bird sent from Noah's Ark. In Scandinavian mythology, the god Odin has a raven sitting on each shoulder. They whisper in his ears all the knowledge of the world.

Our native people call him the Trickster and believe he was instrumental in the creation of the world.

The Raven's lifespan is comparable to that of humans. Their intelligence has been scientifically proven to be five times that of any other bird.

Our tale begins back in 1985 when the government of the day was considering adopting an official territorial bird. pj first broached the subject with a government employee. He became indignant and rejected her suggestion, saying the raven was "not a suitable bird."

Furthermore, it was his sanctimonious opinion that the gray jay (whisky jack) would likely be the bird of choice. He then added insult to injury by stating that the government would simply make an announcement regarding "our" final decision on the Yukon bird.

pj was angry. She knew in her heart that if Yukoners were allowed to choose, they'd pick the raven and not some dreary little gray jay. She complained to then-commissioner Doug Bell who, it turned out, liked the raven idea. Bell agreed to write government leader Chris Pearson expressing concern that the people of the Yukon were not being consulted.

On March 5, the territorial government relented. It was announced that the public was being invited to suggest bird candidates—with two exceptions: The ptarmigan was ruled out because it was already the state bird of Alaska. And the raven was also excluded because it is "a popular choice in a number of areas of North America and Europe, including the Northwest Territories, where it is used widely."

pj was furious. She began to vibrate. She clenched her fists and closed her eyes. Smoke poured from her ears. She was undergoing a metamorphosis that would ultimately change her life. When the smoke cleared, she had been transformed into the Yukon's first Raven Maniac.

pj kicked off her campaign at Horwood's Office Supplies where she posted a petition urging the government to rethink its decision to blacklist the raven from the list of choices. People flocked to sign it.

She then took her campaign to the airwaves. Whitehorse radio station CKRW held a phone-in poll and 80 percent of callers supported the raven.

One woman berated the bird because of its garbage can image. Another praised it as a more efficient sanitary engineer than those employed by the city.

The issue hit the editorial pages of both the *Whitehorse Star* and the *Yukon News* with an avalanche of letters, cartoons and articles. Some were serious, but many spoofed the issue with poems by "Raven W. Service, bird of the Yukon." The bard would have loved it.

It was a volatile issue to be sure. People either loved ravens or hated them. There was no in-between. Regardless of their opinions, people seemed to enjoy putting aside the troubles of the day and having some fun at the expense of the government.

Artist Jim Robb took up the cause. He and pj created Muskeg the Raven buttons which proclaimed the now famous call-to-arms: *"I'm a Raven Maniac!"* They sold like hotcakes.

pj occupied a booth at the sixth annual Yukon Trade Show where she lobbied support and added hundreds of names to her growing petition. She was rewarded by her fans with a personalized licence plate that read: "RAVEN."

In April 1985 the government ate crow. Then renewable resources minister Bill Brewster announced that the raven was indeed eligible as one of ten finalists for Official Bird status. Deadline for nominations was April 30th.

Suddenly the story went national. On April 10th CBC Radio Canada broadcast a news item on The World at Six and letters began filling pj's mailbox from across the country. Even *Toronto Field Naturalists Magazine* wanted the story.

Meanwhile, back in Whitehorse, falcon fanciers, chickadee cheerleaders, raven maniacs and grosbeak boosters were battling it out in the Great Bird Debate. Whitehorse resident Pat Shearer nominated her neighbor's pet budgie Schmengie because "he is a transient, not born here, representing a large percentage of the Yukon's population."

11

Boreal bigotry reared its ugly head. A chickadee cheerleader slammed pj's campaign in the *Yukon News* as "the desperate efforts of one or two mind-manipulating zealots."

pj cried fowl!

A gray jay jester praised the whisky jack because, "like the Conservative government in the Yukon, he always acts friendly toward everyone to receive more free handouts." An eagle enthusiast trashed the raven as "a guzzling black garburator" while a Haines Junction woman suggested the government drop its bird idea altogether and elevate the mighty mosquito as official Yukon symbol. (She was later declared unfit to stand trial.)

As the eleventh hour approached, Raven Maniacs got a boost from a Fort Nelson woman who wrote the *Star* to announce that the B.C. town's council had recently voted to make the "resourceful raven" its official logo.

On April 30th, pj presented her forty-seven page petition to then government leader Willard Phelps. It contained the names of 1,753 Yukon residents who favored the raven.

Phelps played it cool. He said his cabinet would make its decision in late May. He even refused to divulge his own personal preference rather than risk ruffling any more feathers.

But it was too late. Feathers had already been ruffled in Yellowknife where the Chamber of Commerce had used Raymond the Raven sitting on a gold brick as its logo since 1959. Raymond has since appeared on chamber letterhead, buttons, pins and certificates.

When Raymond's mate Ramona Raven appeared before council, the city fathers agreed to appoint her "raven in residence." The city went even further, putting the black mascot on litter baskets. Even *The Yellowknifer* newspaper had incorporated the raven as the central character in its editorial cartoon, masthead, shirts and hats. In doing so, the newspaper claimed to have reproduced more ravens than the ravens themselves.

Magpies were mortified. Ducks were dumbfounded. Bushtits were baffled. The king of garbage cans was now the subject of a tug-of-war between two northern cities that challenged each other for raven rights.

In editorial and news stories, *The Yellowknifer* charged the Yukon with "raven-knapping." Not to be outdone, pj pointed out that the government of the Northwest Territories had adopted a three-legged polar bear as its official symbol.

Back in the Yukon, an election campaign was heating up for a May 13th vote and the raven issue livened up the campaign. In the end, Phelps' Conservatives got plucked and the New Democrats ruled the roost under government leader Tony Penikett. At the new leader's inaugural press conference, the first question asked of Penikett was whether or not the raven was going to be the territorial bird.

"No comment," was his firm reply.

On June 17th the NDP cabinet designated the raven as the Yukon's official bird and legislation was drafted for the fall session of the legislative assembly.

"The raven is an extremely significant bird of the native culture and folklore of the Yukon," said then-justice minister Roger Kimmerly in making the announcement.

"It is an intelligent, independent bird who lives by its wits. We thought it personified and represented the Yukon spirit. It was an easy decision for the cabinet to make." He made the announcement at the Skookum Jim Friendship Center in downtown Whitehorse, chosen because of the raven carvings which adorn the outside of the building.

pj was ecstatic. "This can be realized as a moment in Yukon history when the people spoke and the government listened," she said.

Chickaadees were choked. Schmengie went into seclusion and the rest of the birdies went the way of the Boreal Blue-butted Dodo.

The irony of this story is that so many people worked themselves into a flap over this issue while the ravens themselves remained blissfully unaware to it all.

Life has returned to normal for the people of the Yukon. The Great Bird Debate is now history and the raven reigns supreme as he has done from the dawn of civilization. As far as the raven is concerned nothing has changed. He remains Lord of all he scans.

A First Word

Come drift with me and forget for just a little while your cares and worries as we journey northward to the Land of the Midnight Sun. Relax and share with me some of the wonders of her majesty and the mystery of her lure. She's enchanting. She's waiting. She's calling....

The North I Know

My quest to paint the Yukon's face
In words quite makes me nervous
I'm haunted by Jack London's grace
And awed by Robert Service
They mined the North in words of worth
So brazenly aesthetic
That anything I think to add
Sounds hopelessly pathetic

The tales they told were solid gold
And still today repeated
They said it all with grit and gall
And so I sit defeated
So I must write the North I know
The Yukon of today
The Sourdough of modern times
The lure that makes him stay

The Terror of the North

On August 17 1896 when the cry of *"Gold!"* rang out across Bonanza Creek touching off the exodus of 100,000 greed-struck miners to the Klondike Gold Fields, a shady character by the name of Soapy Smith wasted little time sailing up to the Alaskan port of Skagway to engage in every conceivable form of sham and trickery in order to divest returning miners of every last flake of gold in their pokes.

With the aid of his notorious gang of thugs and shysters and without ever setting foot in the Klondike, Smith soon became a prosperous, albeit much-despised man. Today, Jefferson Randolf 'Soapy' Smith's brief reign of terror remains a legend in the North.

The Ballad of Soapy Smith

Now Soapy Smith was a renegade
Form the 'Lower 48'
Who headed forth to the frozen North
In eighteen ninety-eight
Crazed by news of the Klondike
Half-mad for a poke full of gold
He boarded a ship to Skagway
To find the Mother Lode
And there by the mighty Chilkoot
In the shade of the Gold Rush Trail
He mined the miner's pockets
And found his Holy Grail
Was it whiskey, cards or women
Soapy always aimed to please
With a mindfull of vice and a toss of the dice
He was 'King of the Golden Fleece'

For Smith and his crew of con-men
Were the slime of the human race

The biggest band of scoundrels
Ever gathered in one place
And the dice were always loaded
And the whiskey watered down
As he rose to fame and gained the name
"Most Hated Man in Town"

But Soapy's days were numbered
And his dirty work was done
When he met Frank Reid as fate decreed
On the business end of a gun
Four shots rang out in the harbor
Two bodies fell by the warf
One fearless man of morals
One terror of the North

Now a tombstone stands in the graveyard
Tis a monument to the deed
Of a man who gave his life to end
The reign of a ruthless fiend
Yet a puny slab unhallowed
Has become the mark of fame
Where people come to honor the scum
That brought the town to shame

What's a Sourdough?

The term 'Yukon Sourdough' hails back to the days of the Klondike Gold Rush when a pinch of sourdough batter was religiously saved in a glass jar to serve as leavener for the next batch of bread.

Over the years the term has come to mean a longtime Northerner as opposed to 'Cheechako' or 'newcomer.' A lesser-known definition refers to a person who is 'soured on the country' and has 'no dough' to leave.

The life of a Sourdough is often one of extremes. Summers in the North are incredibly brief, (some claim we only get two seasons: winter and July), for all too soon the days grow short, the leaves begin to change color, and sometimes as the temperature starts to drop we find ourselves wondering—just what is it that keeps us here anyway?

The following poem was inspired by a friend of mine.

My Friend the Sourdough

Well she thought she was a leaver
My friend the Sourdough
And I could not believe her
Until she packed to go

She said
    "I hate this Yukon
    It's such a crazy land
    No other place is like it
    I hope you understand"

I harried to restrain her
But soon I came to know
That nothing would detain her
She couldn't wait to go!

18

She said:
"I hate the flavor
Of winter's somber song
So I'll be on my way for
I know I don't belong

Where nights can last forever
And winter stays so long
I think my plan is clever
I know I can't go wrong

I sure won't miss the Malemutes
That howl on frosty nights
The bears—the Cabin Fever
The snow—the Northern Lights!"

And so she left the Northland
And broke her Yukon tether
In letters later coming forth
She said she loved the weather
The sights in San Francisco
The sun in Mexico
And:
"Baby let me tell ya
The *South's* the place to go!"

Well our letters slowly faltered
Til soon we didn't write
Our paths had simply altered
—Yet something wasn't right
Her absence quite appalled me
Her obstinence I hated
Then yesterday she called me
And spoke so damned elated!

She said:
"I love the Yukon!
It's such a crazy land
No other place is like it
I think you understand"

She said:
"I miss the flavor
Of winter's somber song
Forget my past behavior!
I know where I went wrong

For how I miss the Malemutes
That howl on frosty nights
The bears—the Cabin Fever
The snow—the Northern Lights

I thought I'd gone forever
To join the Southern throng
But—so much for the weather
I know where I belong

I've seen a lot of places
Been dazzled by it all
Yet nothing quite replaces
The lure of Yukon's call

The rat race of the city
Has turned me rather blue
It's such an awful pity
To waste good friends like you"

There's sights in San Francisco
And sun in Mexico
But—baby let me tell ya
The *North's* the place to go!

Children of the Land

Here in the North some children live in town where they pretty much have all the modern amenities, while other children live out in the bush—practise a more traditional lifestyle. I think of my younger brother and sister who were raised out on the trapline and about the life they lived. Their real names are Jeff and Ruby but we called them 'Dibs n' Ribs,' and even though they're pretty much all grown up now I still tend to think of them as 'children of the land.'

The following poem, inspired by my younger brother and sister, was one of my first poems.

Dibs n' Ribs

Once upon a mountain
Beneath the Midnight Sun
There lived a lady trapper
Who had a little son
She also had a daughter
(These lines contain no fibs)
I know for I'm their sister
We called them 'Dibs n' Ribs'
Two chubby little babies
Dark eyes and raven hair
Toddling o'er the mountains
Raised on grizzly bear
One without the other
You'd very seldom see
They roamed the hills together
And each knew every tree
You'd see them in their parkas
At fifty-nine below
Mushing by with dog teams
And laughing in the snow

They're off to check the trapline
As Northern Lights ignite
The Yukon is their playland
This frosty winter night

Little Ribs with rabbit skins
At night beneath her head
Fat Husky pups for teddy bears
To cuddle soft in bed
Lulled by howling Huskies
And counting mountain sheep
They'd snuggle up together
And soon be fast asleep

A pint-size Davy Crockett
My little brother Dibs
He'd site a moose then stalk it
Then haul it home to Ribs
Who'd roast it in the cookstove
As Dibs would never fail
To tell of how he'd shot it
And drug it by the tail

On snowmobile or snowshoe
They'd little time for rest
Two busy little scholars
Of the wilderness
Though youth is but a moment
—A snowflake in your hand
Dibs n' Ribs will e'er to me
Be children of the land

Paradise Gained

My mother lives in a cozy little cabin nestled at the foot of a mountain by a lake in the Yukon wilderness. She is a trapper, game guide, and outfitter known as the Horse Woman.

Her guest ranch is the gathering place for tourists, hunters, and weekend cowboys seeking adventure though high alpine country via horseback in summer and dog team during winter. Her humble abode is home to scores of Malemutes and Huskies, horses of every color, make and model, and a large number of stray cats.

Mother's Little Cabin

Beneath a radiant sunset
High on lonely hill
Where stilted pine trees shiver
And Arctic air is still
Amid a panorama
Of snow-capped Yukon peaks
Lies Mother's Little Cabin
The paradise she seeks

And there amid such splendor
My mother's cabin lies
She has no dues to render
She owns the sapphire skies
The twinkling stars, the Yukon moon
No thief can ever take them
There is no tax on Nature's facts
And all are free to stake them

First Class Turkey

In 1985 when I lobbied the government to recognize the northern raven as the Yukon's official symbol, artist Jim Robb and I designed an official *"I'm a Raven Maniac!"* campaign button that featured a cartoon character by the name of Muskeg the Raven. A thousand buttons went on sale for a buck a button and went like hotcakes, selling out within a week. The design was even pirated by some enterprising soul (miraculously turning up on T-shirts in a store window) and several people offered to buy the one I wore on my jacket for ten bucks.

Muskeg the Raven

He is scruffy and he's quirky
He's a first class Yukon Turkey
Always squawking as he's flying back and forth
He is Muskeg the Raven and he's ever misbehavin'
He's the 147th fastest bird
In the North

His bill is cracked and wrinkled
And he molts the whole year through
His tattered scarf is flapping in the air
Be sure your head is covered
If he's flying over you
Or you might receive a 'Muskeg Souvenir'

He is Lord of all he scans
The king of garbage cans
At fifty-nine below he proves his worth
He's fillin' up his cache stand
With everybody's trash and...
He's the 147th fastest bird
In the North

The Ultimate Sourdough

Although he is often referred to by the ignoble moniker the "common raven," the northern raven has been scientifically proven to be the most intelligent bird alive today on the earth. Unlike in some European cultures that associate Raven with death, Canadian Pacific Northwestern culture recognizes Raven as the celebrated symbol of life and creation and the undisputed hero of myth and legend.

Famous for his dauntless spirit and brazenly oblivious to the severity of the Arctic elements, Raven is truly the Ultimate Sourdough. According to native legend he is called the Trickster, the name suits him well. Who else do you see out wandering around in bare feet when it's sixty below, with enough sense of humor to playfully dive-bomb the neighbor's Husky dog?

Raven is an omnivorous non migratory bird of prey with a life span equal to that of most humans, and is often seen around town during winter months, demonstrating the ancient art of Garbage Can Sabotage. This diet appears to serve him well for, as many a newcomer is amazed to note, he out-sizes his Southern relatives by a phenomenal degree. Affectionately called the Yukon Turkey, I sometimes think of Raven as the Mockingbird of the North as he possesses the ability to imitate a variety of sounds from the jake brake on a semi truck to the voice of a human being.

With an incredible strength of spirit, an admirable sense of humor in the face of adversity, and a personality that is best described as sheer guts n' gumption, this amazing creature is clearly an excellent role model for his human cousins.

The following poem was read in the Yukon legislature in 1985 by former Minister of Justice The Honorable Roger Kimmerly on the occasion of the second reading of Bill #12, "The Raven Act," at which time the Northern Raven became the Yukon's official territorial bird.

Behold the Yukon Raven

Behold the Yukon Raven
Phoenix of the North
Screeching bold obscenities
And strutting back and forth
Upon a cabin rooftop
So fearless. So aloof
Titan bird of Northland
Immune to man's reproof

Glossy black and cocky
A renegade, no doubt
Scrounging through the garbage
He strews it all about
He loves to tease the Huskies
It gives him great delight
To pester them and rob them
Then steal away in flight

In dark and dead of winter
At sixty-nine below
There be a striking absence
Of man and beast and foe
Save for the stalwart raven
There's few will venture forth
As chill and deathly silences
Prevail upon the North

Some say he is intrepid
—Ridiculously bold
Perched upon a lamppost
Defying wind and cold
Scruffy wretched vagrant
He's quick to spot a scrap
This crusty molting scavenger
Who seldom takes a nap

Behold the Yukon Raven
Bird of guile and wit

He screams aloft to shock you
Then swift away he'll flit
Behold his madcap antics
Pray learn from this display
And neither shun the Raven
Who knows not work from play

Where's My Parka?

A stroll through modern day Dawson City is much like walking onto the set of an old western movie. Many false-fronted buildings line her dusty streets; some recently restored to original glamour while others lean drunkenly at odd angles as they quietly sink back into the muskeg upon which they were built.

In summer the town is vibrant and the days are literally endless as the Midnight Sun slowly circles above a bustle of tourists come to recapture the Spirit of 98. But the season is all too brief and before the average Sourdough can say, "Where's my parka?" the streets are deserted, the lawn mower's buried somewhere beneath a snowdrift, and the sun is fading back into a coma. The personality of the North is anything but subtle....

Dawson Winter

A stillness grips Dawson
As winter so awesome
Paints desolate streets iron grey
The trees are a shimmer
Of frost-covered glimmer
   —It's 20 below out today

As winter advances
And lowers the chances
Of catching a sunlit ray
The children in parkas
Go forth in the darkness
   —It's 30 below out today

The mist-colored greylight
That passes for daylight
Is poor light for showing the way
And only the Raven
Appears from his haven
   —It's 40 below out today

The frostbite that's bitten
The hand in the mitten
Is proof of the price that we pay
In seeking relief for
Our dread Cabin Fever
   —It's 50 below out today

With eyelashes frozen
By Nature so cozen
One ventures with little delay
There's none can deny her
And few who defy her
   —It's 60 below out today

The Northwind's a fury
And causes us worry
There's nothing to do now but pray

As Nature spews forth and
We're locked in this Northland
 —It's 70 below out today

So shaded and clouded
And ice fog enshrouded
The town site is fading away
A hand without pity
Has frozen the city
 —It's 80 below out today

But spirits grow stronger
As days nigh grow longer
And winter soon falls by the way
The sun casts a shadow
And oh, we are glad though...
 —It's 90 below out today

Southern Delicacies

Sometimes in the dead of winter when I am out walking in the hills and the sudden breeze of a warm Chinook runs its fingers through my hair, I am apt to dream of faraway places....

Chinook

the warm Chinook
whispers
of palm trees
tropical flowers
perennial sunshine
neverending sunsets
and othersuch
southern delicacies
untransplantable

Is He Laughing at Me or Saying Hello?

Yes, it's just another lazy Northern October Sunday morning here in the Land of the Midnight Sun. As a raven chortles pleasantly somewhere off in the distance, you savor the last few moments of a leisurely sleep-in before finally dragging yourself out of bed and over to the window to greet the dawn of a new day.

As you drink in the sheer beauty of your surroundings you shake your head and sigh, trying to imagine people in noisy overcrowded cities waking up to choke on pollution with every breath. But the minute you gaze over at your neighbor's chimney and see smoke rising straight up in a column like an erect soldier standing at attention, you know you're in trouble.

Suddenly you remember you're right out of coffee—and since you didn't bother to plug in the car last night, chances are it's not gonna budge. And you realize the can of Pepsi you left sitting on the front seat has probably exploded by now—and of course the heat tapes aren't turned on yet so the plumbing's either froze up or one of the pipes is about to burst any minute... and you can't remember where the #?@&* you left your parka... and suddenly you regret putting off getting in this year's firewood because you know this is precisely the morning the old chain saw is likely to go on the fritz....

And as you reluctantly crawl into your scratchy old long woolen underwear and slide into your mukluks, and the annoying rasp of an obnoxious Raven jangles down from the top of a tall jack pine to rattle around inside your brain, you wonder—is he laughing at me or saying hello?

Yes, it's just another lazy Northern October Sunday morning here in the Land of the Midnight Sun....

sunday morning 41 below

bush folk creep from
beds they sleep on

33

loathe to dash as dash they should
to check the smoldering firebox
and chop a bit more
wood

smoke-stacked columns
rise in volumes
row on row throughout the town
folks inside deplore the weather
cabin fever's got them
down

not a mortal
leaves his portal
fearful of the winter gods
throws a dog-gone nother log on
fans the flame and drops to
nod

far-off dusky
chained-up Husky
sings a low lamenting howl
echoing primeval sorrows
nose-to-tail then curls to
scowl

river steaming
ice fog-streaming
crystal clouds of iceberg breath
numbly grasping gasping aspen
bent alee as if in
death

black frost-feathered
winter-weathered
raven stately scans the town
"cool today," he deigns to say
and ruffles up his fluffy
down

Strange Things Done

There are still today many strange things done here in the Land of the Midnight Sun and in Dawson City not long ago there began a rather macabre ritual involving a certain cocktail in which bobbed a 'garnish' of petrified human toe. In an effort to set the record straight regarding the origin of the infamous 'Sour Toe Cocktail' I wrote the following poem.

The Ballad of the Sour Toe Cocktail

You've heard the tale of Sam McGee
And how there's strange things done?
I'll tell you yet a stranger one,
Just give a listen, son

They say there was a miner
So very long ago
Who staggered to his cabin
T'was fifty-nine below
He'd gambled all his gold dust
And drunk a lot of booze
And when he'd got real desperate
He'd gambled off his shoes

He stumbled to his cabin
So numbed by alcohol
He didn't know his toe froze off
He didn't hear it fall
He found it in the morning
Beside the cabin door
And dropped it in his whiskey glass
As solemnly he swore:

"I'll never more taste whiskey
This toe's my souvenir"
He placed it on the mantle top

And shed a silent tear
They say he died of heartbreak
—He'd loved his whiskey so
And went to his heavenly claimstake
And left behind the toe

So—they put it in a cocktail
And many brave Soughdough
Have drunk the booze and without fail
Have left behind the toe
This proved a man of gumption
Though tenderfeet might fidget
To witness a consumption
Wherein there bobbed a digit

Until there came a stranger
From where I do not know
So filled with pride and glassy-eyed
—He swallowed down the toe!
The people up in Dawson
All mourned this tragic loss
And vowed they would replace it
No matter what the cost

They searched the world over
And soon were overjoyed
To find a prairie lady
Whose toe was unemployed
And so they did replace it
But now it's disappeared
I do admit, let's face it
The whole thing's kind of weird

The miner's long forgotten
And tossing in his grave
He's learned the painful lesson
That booze can make you brave
But numbs the mind to danger
Don't you think it's so?
—Just go and ask the stranger
The pain of whiskey's glow!

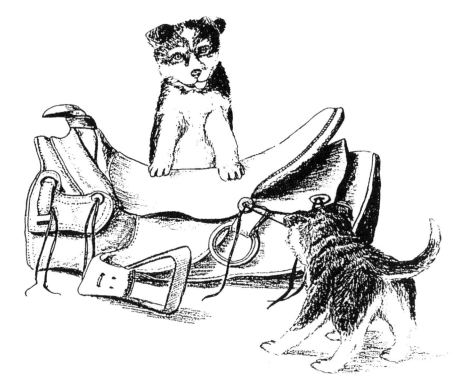

A Thousand Miles of Hell and Ice

I often associate the term 'Sourdough' with the word 'unique' for the people of the North tend to be of a special breed. In a land where individuality is not only welcomed but indeed admired, social boundaries are often vague and it is not uncommon to see a grizzled old bushwhacker standing next to the premier at a social function, the two engaged in animated conversation.

One such individual that comes to mind is Cowboy Larry Smith. The Cowboy is a regular participant in the grueling annual Iditarod sled dog race which is run over 1,049 miles of Alaskan wilderness, beginning in Anchorage and ending at Nome Alaska.

Cowboy Larry Smith

The mushers and their dog teams know
The roughest race on earth
Can break your back and heart and freeze your face
But The Cowboy's Huskies blaze the snow
And ever prove their worth
He lives to mush and always 'sets the pace'

A thousand miles of hell and ice
And forty-nine of tears
From Anchorage Alaska up to Nome
They call the race 'Iditarod'
And all of Yukon cheers
For Cowboy Smith to bring the trophy home

So we salute the Sourdough
Who wears a Stetson hat
And has a will to race much like a thirst
He's number one with us, you know
For Smith knows where it's at
It's how the race is run, not who comes first

On Becoming a Published Poet as the Result of a Locked Door in Clinton Creek....

The town of Clinton Creek first sprang into being in the 1960's when a large deposit of asbestos ore was discovered sixty miles north of Dawson City, Yukon. In the 1970s I worked in this tiny isolated community on the rim of the Arctic Circle driving Uncle Al's Airport Limousine, a little old fifteeen passenger bus, hauling passengers and cargo clanking up the narrow switchbacks to the little red shack at the top of the mountain that served as the airport terminal. A huge sign atop the terminal roof boasted: "Clinton Creek International Airport."

With the depletion of asbestos ore in 1978, signs that Clinton Creek was about to go the way of the small Canadian mining town abounded as families made plans to relocate, buildings were put up for sale and moved from their lots, and the town held a gigantic garage sale.

One afternoon I was packing up dishes in my little trailer when it suddenly hit me that an entire community was about to disappear—forever. Inspired by this thought, I sat down and wrote a poem about the demise of Clinton Creek. Then I tucked it into my pocket and strolled over to the cafeteria and dropped it into the mail slot of the local newspaper, *The Clinton Creek Rock Fluff.*

Then I just stood there for what seemed an eternity, silently staring at the tiny mail slot as an ocean of doubt washed over me. What had I done! Perhaps I was being a bit presumptuous... Maybe there was still a way to get it back! But alas, for the door was locked, the poem was gone, and the dye, as they say, was cast.

Feeling a bit foolish and wondering whatever had possessed me, I slowly turned and walked back to the trailer to finish packing. All thoughts of my brief venture into the world of literature were soon forgotten in a blur of plans and preparation for the family's impending relocation.

A few days before our departure I happened to spot a copy of

the final edition of the town's newspaper and was surprised and delighted to discover my poem printed on the last page. It didn't matter that it was untitled, or even that they had neglected to include my name as author—I had become a published poet!

Clinton Creek Epigram

Well the beer used to flow to the Malemute
And the ore used to flow to the mill
And the bus used to wind up the switch-backs
But everything here is now still

Well the school had its fill of the young ones
The store sold off all of its wares
And the truckers made all of their ore runs
So there's nothing left now but the bears

There were those who were born and who died here
There are memories no one can take
They all laughed and they loved and they cried here
—And got drunk here, for heaven's sake!
Well they even created a lake up
By the mine where the Midnight Sun shone
But then sometime just after last break-up
I looked, and the whole town was gone!

No bunkhouse or store will you find here
The houses are gone from their lots
No snack bar or school left behind here
They only exist in my thoughts

Well they seeded some grass on the tailings
And it looks pretty nice from the ridge
But the cryings and weepings and wailings
When they torn down the Forty mile Bridge!
So now, as you see, there's just me here
I don't mind, but I do miss the past
And the garbage cans that used to be here
...How long can a poor raven last!

Vampire of the North

The malicious nature and colossal dimensions of the Yukon Mosquito is a legend that is occasionally reinforced by the appearance of headlines such as: *"Brave Huntsmen Down 40 Lb Buzzer... Disappointed No New Record Set"* and *"Entire Dog Team Disappears Without A Trace... Mosquitos Suspect."*

Although these bloodthirsty little vampires seem intent on exterminating the entire Sourdough race, it is encouraging to note that to date they have had only minimal success. Even so, safety-minded tourists are advised to keep a close eye on toddlers and small pets during their stay here in the North.

The Truth About Mosquitos

You lay your weary head down
You're nearly fast asleep
You hear a pesty buzzing
So from the bed you leap
You take a rolled up paper
And swat the little mite
And think that you are safer
—Don't be so sure you're right

The sly female mosquito
Is silent as she lights
And as you lie asleep —oh!
She'll take a dozen bites
The male will only buzz you
(He's not akin to violence)
So only fear because you
Have heard a bit of *silence*

Fact or Fiction?

A familiar sight on the streets of Whitehorse until his death in
1977 was Wigwam Harry Fiecke. Wigwam was a merry soul
whose life in all probability will not be chronicled in Yukon
history books, however 'Wiggy' was a most memorable fellow,
noted for his flamboyant manner and unconventional lifestyle.
The following poem was inspired by actual events of his life.

Wigwam Harry Fiecke

Swingin' round the lamppost
Dancin' down the street
There goes the sprightly spirit
Of Wigwam Harry Fiecke

When Harry was a younger man
In nineteen-forty-two
He helped to build the Alcan
But this is known to few

A salty, spry, and boyish rogue
Is what we most remember
Who loved to blaze the night away
Unto a dying ember

He loved the taste of Yukon Hootch
And wine and song and women
And dreamed of whiskey rivers
That were warm enough for swimmin'

He dreamed of islands desolate
Where no one lived but Harry
And fifty lovely Yukon maids
All begging him to marry

With little use for finery
And lesser use for clocks

One day he made his home inside
A big piano box

And there in Sleepy Hollow
He lay his weary head
Til someone told the Mounties

"A Man is down there... dead!"
Now the Redcoats always got their man
And so they started walkin'
They startled weary Harry so
He cried, "Next time try knockin'!"

"...A man can't get no privacy!
    Have you no reverence?"
And so the Mounties closed the case
For lack of evidence

He'd many friends in Whitehorse town
Although I must relate here
Some people thought him rather strange
For living in a crate here

A pal once knocked on Harry's 'door'
Then heard old Harry boom:
"Jest hold yer shirt, I'm on my way
—I'm in the other room!"

And Harry was a diggin' man
No diggin' man was greater
For few were made could swing a spade
Like 'Fiecke the Excavator'

Basements, cellars, post holes too
He shovelled like a miner
He'd shovel if you asked him to
A hole straight through to Chiner!

To dig a basement Harry was
Once hired by a client
And Harry took the job because
He thought the man reliant

But when there came the end of day
And Harry's work completed
He found his boss refused to pay
And Harry felt deceited

As dander rose from head to toes
He hatched his resolution
That spade-by-spade, his boss be paid
By act of restitution

The devil drove his spade that night
His shovel flew like lightnin'
Old mattresses and tires too
Were tossed in 'for the heightnin'

When on his work the dawn did grace
One basement had diminished
Great piles of rubble filled its space
And Harry's work was finished!

A liberated man was he
Who sallied forth undaunted
No matter what the world might think
He lived the way he wanted

Though now he's gone
Still late at night
There roves the ghost of Harry
Way down in Sleepy Hollow
Raisin' hell and makin' merry!

Together Today for Our Children Tomorrow

The year 1994 marks the twenty-first year since respected elder, the late Elijah Smith first started the ball rolling on Yukon native land claims. In 1988, inspired by his famous call-to-arms: "Together Today for Our Children Tomorrow," I wrote a poem called *reclaiming*.

As an annual performer at the Northern Storytelling Festival in Whitehorse every year I conclude my performance with a recitation of reclaiming, accompanied by the rhythm of a moose hide drum and I have made a personal commitment to continue to do so for as long as it takes Yukon land claims to finally become a reality.

In the Yukon, First Nations are divided into two moieties, or clans: the Wolf Clan and the Crow (or Raven) Clan, hence the Yukon is often referred to as the Land of the Wolf and Crow.

The following poem touches on the issue of Yukon native land claims and the idea behind it is that you cannot claim something that is already yours. You can only reclaim it.

reclaiming

    the spirit of Raven is rising
    the Wolf howls out to the moon
    the day is ripe for honor
    as lonely weeps the loon

the land cries out to the people
the people cry out to the land
what price for the soul of the Wolf and Crow
does anyone understand?
what price for the ancestral homeland
what debt is there need to repay
what ease for the loss of a heritage
that never was given away?

as the stream knows its path to the ocean
the caribou knows where to roam
as each star knows its place in the darkness
a people must know a home
as the crocus knows when to be purple
the salmon knows when it must spawn
so the sleeping bear wakes in the springtime
to reclaim its place in the sun

Food for Thought

Although the use of fur is sometimes frowned on in some parts of today's modern world according to the dictates of certain popular social trends, the harvesting of wild animals in the Canadian North is not only a traditional way of life dating back millennia and preceding the advent of the European, it is the very foundation upon which this country was built—a fact clearly reflected by our national symbol, the Canadian beaver.

In today's world of intolerance it is important to recognize that the basic elements of survival required for an office worker living in Vancouver are vastly different from those of the Inuit hunter in the high Arctic where a pair of fur-lined mukluks can mean the difference between life and death at subzero temperatures.

For hundreds of thousands of years the hunting and trapping of wild game in the Canadian North has been a primary source of the survival of its people. Within Northern culture there is deep respect for all living things. Whenever game is taken, the hunter first offers a prayer of thanks to the animal for sacrificing its life in order to sustain the lives of the hunter and his family. Then all portions, including flesh, bone, sinew, hide, and claws are used to provide food, clothing, tools, utensils, jewelry and works of art, and it is a mark of respect that no part of the animal is left to go to waste.

In contemplating the honor and wisdom inherent in this admirable way of life, one is tempted to draw comparisons and wonder, for example—how many people think to pause and extend a word or two of thanks to the Christmas turkey they are about to consume before they reach for the carving knife? Food for thought, indeed!

The following poem was inspired by my mother who is a Yukon trapper. It is a playful tribute to her way of life and I tend to think of it as my autobiographical piece.

Yukon Trapper's Daughter

Well I was born a Yukon trapper's daughter
In a cabin by a creek with runnin' water
We were poor but we had gloves
That's just one thing my Momma made fur of
She traded pelts to make
A trapper's dollar

In the midnight sun we often had hares to snare
But in the wintertime she'd knock down a grizzly bear
That was hangin' around in the bush
An' then the next day she'd knock down a moose
Momma always managed to find
The shotgun somewhere

Momma loved and raised us kids on a trapper's pay
She hung our clothes out to freeze-dry everyday
Why I've seen her fingers freeze
Without a parka she's choppin' down trees
But Momma's smile is always frozen
On her face

Well nothin' much has changed since god knows when
An' I doubt if much will ever change again
Not the Yukon. Not the North.
Not Momma's Stetson, not even her horse
Guess I'll always be a Yukon
Trapper's daughter

Yeah I'm proud to be a Yukon trapper's daughter
I remember well the way to skin an otter
Well I stock the woodstove at night
And mush the Huskies by the Northern Lights
Cause I was born to be a Yukon
Trapper's daughter

I guess I'll always be a Yukon
Trapper's daughter

Inside or Out?

People who have never travelled beyond the 60th parallel tend to view the North with a certain mystique, while Northerners in isolated communities often refer to anyplace south of 60 as Outside. The genuine Sourdough is a non migratory species, proud to call one of the most beautiful and unspoiled places in Canada home.

Long Live the Sourdough!

There's frost upon the window
There blows a northern gale
And some say "Here comes winter!"
And some say "Here comes jail!"
For winter in the Yukon
Continues all year round
Save for two months of summer
So short as to astound

The north is full of wonder
And certainly extremes
With pageantry eccentric
She's bursting at the seems
She never gives out samples
And seldom is she shy
With bold austere examples
She glares you in the eye

The twining birch is quaking
She sways as if to bow
Leafless, cold and shaking
The winter from her brow
Do snowflakes falls from heaven?
I see them drifting down
Like grim eternal leaven
Distorting summer ground

The mercury coerces
The sun to hibernation
It's winter in the Yukon
With little hesitation!
A ghastly cloud of ice fog
Obscures what precious view
Of Yukon sun allotted
As winter venoms spew

Some huddle in their cabins
As others flee 'Outside'
While some don furry parkas
With relish undenied
And mock old Mother Nature
For many times they've faced
The war of wills she wages
Upon the bitter waste

They go their way despite her
As sub degrees impend
And yearn but to requite her
For Northern Lights she'll send
With hearty jubilation
They welcome forth the snow
They are the salt of Yukon
—Long live the Sourdough!

The Ghost of Jack London

The following is a true story about the ghost of Jack London that first appeared in *The Yukon Reader* magazine accompanied by a note written by editor Sam Holloway that read in part:

> I too saw Jack London's ghost. Twice. The first time, I was parked across from his cabin (late fall, 1985) in my old van, rolling a cigarette. I glanced over at the cabin to see a figure waving at me from the glassless window. He wore a white shirt and had a hairdo like Jack Kennedy. I dropped my makings on the floor and looked away. When I looked back the figure was gone.
>
> Another time, dead winter, 1986 fifty below, midnight, I strolled past Jack London's cabin, my feet crunching on the frozen snow. This time I heard a voice coming from the cabin; male, rather high-pitched. The same figure waved at me from the window frame. It glowed with a phosphorescent light and I kept walking. By that time I was quite used to seeing ghosts in Dawson City.

The Ghost of Jack London's Cabin

Does the ghost of Jack London continue to haunt a little cabin way up in the Yukon? Has the author of such classics as *White Fang* and *Call of the Wild* somehow found his way back from the other side to settle in a place that is now little more than a ghost town? Perhaps I'll just tell the story and let you decide for yourself.

The story really begins on that fateful day of August 17, 1896, when the cry of *"Gold!"* rang out on Bonanza Creek, sending some 100,000 Argonauts stampeding to the tiny strip of Yukon swampland known as Dawson City, Yukon. Jack London was one such Argonaut. He boarded a steamer in San Francisco, and made his way North to try his hand at gold mining, toughing out the long dark winter months in a little cabin out on Henderson Creek.

London survived in the North for less than a year. Apparently concluding that his pen was his gold mine, he bought himself a ticket on the first southbound riverboat the following spring. Before his departure he paused long enough to carve his signature into a log at the back of his humble abode and headed back to San Francisco where he went on to become a world-famous author.

Years later in 1969, the cabin was rediscovered, dismantled and hauled into Dawson City where it was divided in two. Half the cabin was then shipped down to London's birthplace in Oakland California, and the other half was reassembled at the site in Dawson City where it remains to this day, forever abandoned by its distinguished former inhabitant. Or so they say....

You see, back in 1981 I was living in Dawson City, directly across the street from the London Cabin. My two youngest daughters, who were approximately nine and ten years old at the time, decided the cabin would make a great playhouse, and immediately took up residence; toting dolls, teddy bears, and even a small table and chair set across the street. I never thought too much about it; it was handy, I always knew where they were, and all I had to do was lean my head out the window to call them in for supper.

At some point in early spring of that year, unbeknownst to me, they hit upon the idea of playing Sunday school in there. Armed with Bibles, songbooks, and a big bag of chocolate chip cookies, they lured their little friends over to the cabin to attend their first revival meeting—turned out to be quite the affair.

Once the little congregation had assembled in the cabin, the two well-meaning soul-savers proceeded to introduce Jesus to the lot of them. They began by conducting a little Fire and Brimstone sermon, detailing the downward and disastrous fate of children who didn't get themselves saved, and all about how the Devil was down there, just waitin' to roast you to a crisp if you didn't pay attention.

Now, if you wanted to get yourself saved, they said, the best way to get started was with a bit of prayin.' So the eager converts gathered in a circle, bowing their heads, and the prayers began in earnest. The two Evangelists appeared to be making some headway.

Headway, that is, until a fierce stomping and banging on the cabin roof suddenly interrupted things.

The entire congregation freaked and tore out the door like a shot, the two soul-savers bringing up the rear. And that might well have been the end of it right then and there, had not the two determined Evangelists pointed out that it was probably just some neighbor kids playing a joke. Why, they might even still be around somewhere—why don't we take a look? (The possibility of salvaging a few more souls suddenly loomed on the horizon.)

They proceeded to circle the cabin, ploughing their way single file through two- and three foot-high snowdrifts, hoping to discover.... Well they weren't quite sure just what. No sign of anyone. Not so much as a footprint. They trudged down the path a bit to get a better view of the cabin roof—about two feet of snow up there. Likewise undisturbed.

Some members of the congregation began to express reservation about the prospect of reentering the cabin but were soon persuaded to join in resuming services; partly by the suggestion that "the stomping and banging just might have been a message from above that they were in serious need of gettin' themselves saved," and partly by mention of the chocolate cookie feast that was to take place immediately following services.

And so it was that the innocent little flock slowly filed back into the cabin to take their places. It was decided that order would be restored with the singing of a few good old church songs. They began with a moving rendition of Amazing Grace, singing the first verse three times in a row, since no one knew the rest of the words. That worked out so well they went right on into Jesus Loves Me.

The two church leaders couldn't help but feel a pious sense of accomplishment as they gazed out across the glowing faces of the little congregation. A word of thanks seemed quite in order before breaking open the bag of chocolate chip cookies. All were instructed to bow their heads and a heartfelt prayer was offered to The Man Upstairs, as they had fondly come to refer to Him.

And a fine prayer it was, too; thanking parishioners for their faith, and of course, The Lord for His most gracious bounty of which they were about to partake. They were just about at the Amen part when a thundering *Crash! Crash! Crash!* suddenly shook the cabin roof.

This time the entire congregation, now terrified out of its

mind, tore out of there like greased lightening, screeching, "Help! Help! It's the Devil!" Even the two Evangelists took to their heels, hollering at the top of their lungs, "Run for your lives!" leaving teddy bears, Bibles, and the bag of chocolate chip cookies far behind.

Now, as the parent of four busy young preadolescents, I'm pretty much used to the odd antic; someone's forever getting themselves into hot water. If it isn't one, it's the other something gets accidently broken, somebody flushes something down the toilet that shouldn't go down there, someone decides the cat needs a haircut.... I've pretty much seen it all. But I must admit, it's not everyday I see the two youngest come smokin' through the door, white as a sheet with their eyes bulging and their hair standing on end.

"Okay, so what's up?" I ask. No one says anything. Just stand there with their teeth chattering. "Hey there, cat got your tongue? What's wrong with you two?" They just stand there, staring.

Three whole days pass by and not a word out of either of them. Finally I ask them why they never seem to want to go out and play anymore and out pops the whole story, with both of them chattering away a mile-a-minute, the youngest finally winding down with: "We're not lying, Mom," and gazing skyward to add most reverently, "honest to God."

"Alright, you two," I say, "we'll go over there tomorrow and pack up the rest of your belongings."

"N-uh-uh!" they howl. "We're never going in there again, *ever*! Everyone says that place is haunted."

And that was pretty much the end of it—just like that; two potentially bright careers in religion cruelly snuffed out, and one playhouse, abandoned forever. Well, almost forever. I went upstairs to look out my bedroom window. There across the street stood the little cabin, looking kind of old and lonely. Full two feet of snow on the roof... undisturbed. "Hmmm," I thought, "s'pose there really are some strange things done in the Midnight Sun... not to mention the winter moon."

The next day I ventured across the street. It was dark inside the cabin, but the place had an air of calmness about it—almost a kind of serenity. As I loaded up dolls, teddy bears, chocolate cookies and the like, the wind began to howl around the corners of the cabin and I heard the mournful wail of a Malemute begin to rise somewhere in the distance. The hair at the back of my neck began to bristle, and as I made my way out the door I remarked, "Nice place to visit... wouldn't want to live here—uh, no offence, Jack!"

The kids and their friends continued to refer to the cabin as the Haunted House and shortly after that we moved back down to Whitehorse. One evening a few months later, my good friend, artist Jim Robb was sitting at my kitchen table working on a sketch of Jack London's Cabin when he happened to mention that Jack's mother had been clairvoyant. For some reason I felt a shiver run down my spine. I decided to read up on Jack London.

Turns out that Jack's mother had been a bit strange indeed. Apparently she was heavily into the paranormal. And there was certainly a darker side to London, which may not have been to surprising when you consider that when he was just six years old, his mother used to hold seances at which she would sit Jack on the kitchen table and amuse herself by levitating the table until it floated in the air. Jack's young friends referred to his house as "The Spook House."

London lived out his life a staunch atheist, acquiring, at some point, a bizarre taste for blood-rare ducks (which he enjoyed just barely braised on the outside so that when he gorged himself the blood ran down his face). He became severely addicted to morphine and although there was some controversy regarding the matter, his death by overdose at the age of forty in 1916 had all the earmarks of suicide.

About a year after the strange incident at the cabin I happened to travel up to Dawson City. Just for kicks I dropped by to visit my old digs and then took a stroll across the street to the London Cabin.... Everything looks pretty much the same; little worn path winding up the hill, still no door on the cabin... dirt floor. I walk inside and look up. Look up at the sky, because now there's a gaping hole where the roof has fallen in.

I feel a sudden chill. Scarcely a year ago six young kids had been scared out of their wits because someone or something had been stomping and banging around up there—why hadn't it caved in then? Again I find myself wondering why there hadn't been any sign of pranksters. Something had definitely scared those kids. Could it be possible that Jack was still around—and not at all partial to anyone holding revival meetings here?

I start thinking about how Dawson City is full of old and derelict buildings, built during the Gold Rush, many of which have sunk down into the muskeg so that they lean drunkenly at odd angles (...ah, if only those walls could talk—imagine the stories?). And about how, over the years there've been many reports of ghost sightings; everyone from Klondike Kate to Arizona Charlie....

Gradually I am overtaken with a deep sense of melancholy, my mind flooded with visions of Jack London as he struggled to survive the bitter cold of a long dark winter in a lonely cabin out on Henderson Creek, the thrill of adventure diminishing as he found himself isolated in a foreign land faced with dwindling supplies and disappearing dreams....

"Enough of this!" I laugh and pull up the hood of my parka, waving one arm in a dramatic flourish as I turn to leave—"I bid thee farewell, Mr. London—God rest your soul!"—only to freeze and recoil in horror as the face of Jack London suddenly looms before me in the darkness, its liquid features distorted and bathed in a phosphorescent aura that slowly descends to reveal the figure of a male. My bones turn to ice. Too numb to move, to even breathe, I can only stare in silence as menacing red eyes burn and spit fire.

The figure begins to rise, lifting smoothly, effortlessly, propelled by some invisible force as it glides across the room in a kind of ethereal ballet and pauses to hover by the window. It leans forward cupping its hands as if to blow out a candle then stops abruptly, head tilted to one side and brows knit as though it has spied something on the floor beside the woodstove.

I lower my eyes to follow the direction of its gaze and catch the faint glint of something lying half buried in the dirt floor. The vile taste of horror begins to rise in my throat and an icy fist slowly wraps itself around my heart as I realize I am staring at the rusted handle of a knife.

The figure remains motionless; transfixed, its eyes blood-red with passion. The walls begin to creak and moan; heaving and sighing, ceiling beams crack and shudder above my head. A clamor of raucous laughter rises and fades, ringing in my ears as it thunders across the roof to culminate with a resounding crash that shakes me to my soul and I lean into the wall for support as the entire building begins to rock and sway.

The knife begins to move, turning slowly in the dirt, and I watch with disbelieving eyes as it eases from the earth and rises to hover above my head. Spinning violently, it flies across the room and lodges in a thick log on the back wall of the cabin. Digging itself into the old wood, it slashes and gouges and a series of crooked letters begin to appear. I lean forward straining to read the words. A pungent odor of melted wax suddenly fills my nostrils and my head snaps back to the window.

Nothing is there. The figure is gone. A creak of old hinges. A door opens. Then closes. Then silence.

I shift my gaze to the back of the cabin. The knife too has vanished. Only a few crooked letters remain etched upon the wall. Glowing faintly, they seem to shrink and grow, to beckon me, and I move forward, mesmerized, drawn toward them in some inexplicable way as they gradually blend together to form words. Trancelike, I reach out to touch them and in an instant, they too are gone. Silently I mouth the words: Jack London.

Light appears to reenter the cabin and I look up. Through the gaping hole in the roof the sky is a blaze of indigo, a hint of full moon illuminating stray wisps of cloud. The atmosphere within becomes a warm embrace, all traces of evil seemingly vanished.

Was I going mad? No! No way. I'm not the type. Hell, I don't even believe in ghosts. A figment of the imagination. The mind playing tricks. Ha ha ha. I just happen to have one hell of an imagination. ...still....

"Well, Mr. London," I say taking one last look around, "think I'll just leave you a little souvenir." And I take out my penknife and quickly carve a little cross into a log by the doorway. Then I tear out the door and run like hell! Don't ask me why, I'm still not exactly sure myself!

Honest to God
Amen

Afterword

Curious to know whether the cross I had carved was still intact, I revisited the London Cabin in the summer of 1991 and was surprised to find it now facing the street, dwarfed by an impressive display of London memorabilia. However, I was equally surprised to discover that a wrought iron barricade had been placed over the door to the cabin.

"So much for that idea," I concluded. But then as fate would have it, my old friend Dick North—resident expert on anything pertaining to Jack London—happened to be in attendance and was only too happy to escort me into the cabin.

It was cool and dark inside. Silently cursing the fact that I am extremely nearsighted, I squinted and scanned the old log walls, willing the cross to materialize. But to no avail. It appeared to have vanished mysteriously. Could it all have been a dream? Little more than the conjurings of an overworked imagination compounded by a severe case of Cabin Fever?

I began to lose hope when suddenly my companion (who happened to be blessed with 20/20 vision) smiled and pointed to the right of the doorway. Instantly I recognized the tiny, perfectly formed cross I had carved there ten years previously. A certain satisfaction washed over me; my return to the cabin had been something of a pilgrimage. But I had one final mission to carry out before heading back to Whitehorse.

Later that evening at about midnight I paid a last visit to the cabin. There, with some assistance from my sharp-eyed companion, I climbed onto the roof and made my way across its sod-covered thatch to perch above the doorway and pose for a photograph as the Midnight Sun cast an eerie green shadow across the horizon. What an adventure!—and this time the roof held.

Epilogue

Upon returning home to Whitehorse, I set about getting this story into final draft. I was feeling quite smug. Imagine, a photograph to prove that I'd had the last laugh on London! But alas, for it was not to be.

Almost like a premonition, a strange event occurred. One evening I heard a loud crash in my office and opened the door to discover that a mirror had slipped off the wall and smashed down onto one of my manuscripts—the manuscript containing the story of "The Ghost of Jack London's Cabin." A long shard of glass lay pointed directly at the name printed on the bottom of the last page: my name.

Coincidence? Perhaps. But then the next day I learned that something had gone wrong during the processing of my photographs and the entire film had been destroyed. I decided to have it developed anyway. What emerged was a blurry set of prints detailing a few ghostly images of myself and the cabin. On closer observation I realized that I had been wearing my Dr. Faustus T-shirt. The irony was not wasted on me. The tale of Dr. Faustus is the granddaddy of all the Sell-Your-Soul-to-the-Devil stories.

...the curse of the cross lives on.

A Final Word (Farewell)

And so our journey ends. I hope this brief odyssey into the soul of the Yukon has helped you to capture a little of her spirit. As we slowly drift back to the place of our departure, don't be surprised if you should discover that a trace of her spirit has etched itself indelibly upon your heart, for she is a most unforgettable lady.

Perhaps you are beginning to understand the power of her lure. Perhaps she will tempt you to return. She's enchanting. She's waiting. She's calling.....

Other Hancock House Titles

Robert Service
51/2 X 81/2, 64 pp. SC
ISBN 0-88839-223-0

Robert Service
51/2 X 81/2, 64 pp. SC
ISBN 0-88839-224-9

Jack London
51/2 X 81/2, 104 pp. SC
ISBN 0-88839-259-1

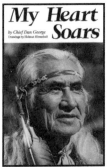

Chief Dan George and
Helmut Hirnschall
51/2 X 81/2, 96 pp. SC
ISBN 0-88839-231-1

Chief Dan George and
Helmut Hirnschall
51/2 X 81/2, 96 pp. SC
ISBN 0-88839-233-8

Mike Puhallo, Brian Brannon,
and Wendy Liddle
51/2 X 81/2, 64 pp. SC
ISBN 0-88839-368-7

Robert F. Harrington
51/2 X 81/2, 96 pp. SC
ISBN 0-88839-367-9

pj johnson
51/2 X 81/2, 64 pp. SC
ISBN 0-88839-366-0

James and Susan Preyde
51/2 X 81/2, 96 pp. SC
ISBN 0-88839-362-8

All titles available from HANCOCK HOUSE PUBLISHERS, 1431 Harrison Ave., Blaine, WA 98230-5005
(604) 538-1114   Fax: (604) 538-2262   Mastercard, Visa, or Check accepted.